THE
HEALER

THE
HEALER

Jean-Marie Vianney Nkusi

ARPress
45 Dan Road Suite 5
Canton MA 02021

| Hotline: | 1(888) 821-0229 |
| Fax: | 1(508) 545-7580 |

Ordering Information:
Quantity sales. Special discounts are available on quantity purchases by corporations, associations, and others. For details, contact the publisher at the address above.

Printed in the United States of America.

| ISBN-13: | Paperback | 979-8-89356-654-3 |
| | eBook | 979-8-89356-655-0 |

Library of Congress Control Number: 2024903684

Contents

Jean-Marie Vianney Nkusi

Jesus loves the little children. He is always there to help them and guide them in the right path. As Children of God, let us welcome Jesus Christ in our lives and let him lead us into Paradise. God bless you,

Evangelist Jean-Marie Vianney Nkusi

Chapter 1

It was mid-night while lying in bed very sick for a very long period of 3 months without going to school. I was in a state of coma. As it was my family tradition of reciting rosary with the whole family every night before going to be, in the refugee camp of Bibwe.

As my state of health was in complete hopelessness. My Spirit was praying to Father God in the Precious name of Jesus Christ. Remember That Jesus Christ was a patron of the little children and believed that he will make a miracle in my life and heal me. I then asked Jesus to smile to me and heal me now. All the sudden as I was calling my mommy and my daddy to come to rescue me for, I was dying.

My spirit started to sing a song called Jesus love the little children, Jesus loves the little children, Jesus loves the little children and suddenly my spirit was taken away in the very beautiful place called Heaven and Jesus Christ came to welcome me smiling and then said Smile my beloved Child Jean- Marie and said do not worry from now for your prayer was hard, you are healed. Jesus Christ holds my hand as he was talking to me in Kinyarwanda telling me how much he loves me. I felt very happy and peaceful. He took me to meet his mother, The Virgin Mary. She was a very beautiful lady. She then joyfully lifted me up and putted me on her laps carefully touching my head and massaging my shoulders and I felt completely healed and very happy.

Chapter 2

HOW I SAW HEAVEN

Heaven is a very beautiful Place. A very bright full of love. No pain and suffering, no sickness and diseases, no hate, no wars, no jealousy, no envy. What you find is joy, Peace and Happiness. It is where people never die, they live forever and ever with our Heavenly father God. When you arrive there, you are change completely and you are given a new body that stays forever. There are no young or old people that you find there, everybody there rejoices before the heavenly throne where Jesus Christ is the great Host and Great King full of Grace.

Chapter 3

MY FIRST ENCOUNTER WITH THE ANGELS

When My Savior Jesus Christ sent me back from heaven to earth, upon my arrival, I was completely free from sickness, suffering and pain. I was rejoicing and thankful to God my Father Who is in Heaven and Jesus Christ my savior Immaculate Conception our lady of Peace Virgin Mary who took care of me while in Heaven. As I was sent by Jesus Christ to life on earth so that I will be a witness of what I saw with my eyes when I was in Heaven. God is love, Praise God. Jesus Christ gave me a message to give to all people of earth that He is Alive and well. Hallelujah to our Heavenly Father God.

My second day on earth free from Malaria sickness on earth there came a visitation of Angels from Heaven sent by Jesus Christ to me to bring me the good news. In my dream, I saw many little children of my age each one was holding a small Bible. The writings in the Bible looked like Hebrew language. We were reading it together. They had different looks. Some look black, white, yellow, red, pink, brown, etc....

They taught me the Holy Scriptures from their small Bibles. We were playing happily together in the backyard of my family home in Ngagara, Bujumbura, Burundi, and Africa where we were refugees from Rwanda.

Chapter 4

THE MESSENGER GOD SENT TO ME, HIS NAME

IS ANGEL GABRIEL

Then came to me a very huge and tall white man dressed in white cloth. He was very good looking. He descended from Heaven and came to me. Then said, may Peace be with you Jean-Marie Nkusi, and my name is Angel Gabriel. God has sent me to you to tell you that He has chosen you to be the leader of your family, this is the good news. He also told me that Jesus Christ loves me, and He will be always there to protect you and provide you with anything that you will ever need. Praise God.

Chapter 5

COPPING WITH LIFE ON EARTH

As I was copping with my life in the normal way on earth again, I lived like any other children of my age, a simple and happy life. I read the holy Bible and prayed to God every day. My family tradition was very religious. We had to pray together every morning and every night before we go to bed. I made mistakes like everybody else, but my hope was in Jesus Christ for whom I turn to in time of distresses. Anytime I would call Him, and He was always there to answer my call. Jesus Christ is my Helper. Mother Mary is always there for me as well. They always come to visit me and provide me of anything that I asked them to give to me. Glory be to God our Father who is in Heaven.

Chapter 6

MY FIRST MINISTRY ON EARTH

My first ministry of Evangelism back on earth when I was 12 years old.

When I started, I had with me a New Testament Bible and used to carry it everywhere I went. I shared the good news of Jesus Christ at school and in Community. I went door to door and nocked, when they open for me, then I great them and said may Peace be with you. After I introduced myself to them and told them that I was coming to share with them the good news of Christ Jesus and prayed with them. It was a very blessing a fantastic experience that I had in those days. With this message of salvation, I gave them, I was filed with power of Holy Spirit and possessed with Heavenly gift of healing.

John 3:16 in the holy bible says like this:

For God so loved the world that his only begotten son Jesus Christ so whosoever believes in him will not perish but have everlasting life, Amen.

Chapter 7

THE GIFT OF HEALING THE SICK

God the Father has given me the many gifts and talents. The most cherishing one is the gift to pray for the sick and be healed in the most precious name of Jesus.

Chapter 8

WITNESSING THE FIRST HEALING MIRACLE

I was a volunteer in a local Hospital called (Hopi tale Prince Louis Charles) located in Bujumbura Burundi. One day in the afternoon in the mental nursing ward, a nurse came pushing a man who was very sick. This man could not eat or drink and was not talking due to this sickness. Every day he was vomiting lots of blood. He was apparently possessed by the evil spirit which kept on beating him all the time. This man was in his 30's. A Burundian national whom at the time was doing business in Mombasa Kenya. One day according to his story he visited a resort City of Kenya, the coast of Mombasa. He met somebody who told him that he can make him very rich. He said that he is taking him some place where this money supposed to be. He accepted the offer, and this stranger took him underground of Indian Ocean. He found himself in a strange place where he met the devil. The devil told him that he will make him very rich but with a condition of not to tell anyone about this. If he revealed to where he got the money, the devil is going to kill him.

Chapter 9

THE MIRACLE AND HEALING OF JEAN-BOSCO

HAKIZIMANA

The spirit of God spoke to me and told me to go to pray for this man for the medical doctors could not find the symptoms of sickness. I went to his hospital bed where he was laying desperately and told him that I come to pray for him, he said yes. I asked him if he knows and believe in Jesus Christ healing miracles written in the Holy Bible. He said He believe in Him. Then I laid my hand on his head and started to seek for Jesus Christ healing miracles on this poor man. Then as I continued to pray, the Holy Spirit visited this place and the man started shaking and the other seek people joined us and prayed with us. It was an amazing moment in this Hospital. I went home and left the Bible with him. I came back the next day and found the man starting to feel better and the blood he was vomiting has completely stopped. The patients were very happy to see me again and told me what they have witnessed all night. They were shouting and glorifying God. We continued to pray, pray, pray. I left and comeback the man was completely healed and rejoicing. I told him not to sin again and told him may Peace of God be with you. I say goodbye to him. One week after the miracle, he came to my home to thank me and asked me if he can give me some money, I Sayed no for what I did for him was from God who used me to pray for him.

Chapter 10

REJOICING AND PRAISING GOD FOR GIFT

HEALING MIRACLE

I prayed for this man Jean-Bosco Hakizimana in the name of Jesus Christ. When he was healed, he told me that he has revealed the secret to someone else and the devil begun to beat him every day and was constantly vomiting blood. He stopped talking due to the satanic beatings.

I continued to cast the demons out of him in the most precious name of Jesus. The complete miracles and healing took 3 days of prayers and the demons in him left him and he was free again. Praise God.

About The Author

Jean-Marie V. Nkusi was born in Uganda after his family was forced to flee the Rwandan revolution because of his father's royal connections and government position. While living in a refugee camp in Burundi, Nkusi had a spiritual awakening that has led him to be the educator, evangelist, and humanitarian that he is today. He is particularly interested in raising money to help malnourished children in Africa and around the world and dedicated to spreading the word that "Jesus loves the little children and us all. He is alive and well. There is no other way that can lead you to Heaven except to follow Jesus the Great King." Today, Jean-Marie is a proud Rwandan Canadian living in Edmonton, Alberta with his wife and four beautiful children.

www.ingramcontent.com/pod-product-compliance
Lightning Source LLC
Chambersburg PA
CBHW060359130626
46553CB00003B/1306